The Ghost Assembly Line

New Women's Voices Series, No. 121

poems by

Sarah Sala

Finishing Line Press
Georgetown, Kentucky

The Ghost Assembly Line

New Women's Voices Series, No. 121

ACKNOWLEDGMENTS

Grateful acknowledgement is made to the editors of publications in which
these poems first appeared:

Atlas Review: "60 Year Slide"
Bodega Magazine: "Twin Moons"
Cactus Heart Press: "Thanksgiving Break 2009"
The Leveler: "Before Much Ado about Nothing"
The Mackinac: "Infinite Fish"
Palimpsest: Yale Literary & Arts Magazine: "Rothko's Boy with Red
Backpack"
Poetry Ireland Review: "Tanager Street"
The Stockholm Review of Literature: "Blue Dog Blue Dog" & "Epigrams for
Dorothy
Vending Machine Press: "Untraceable" & "Poem after Man: Kitchen Table"

Editor: Christen Kincaid

Cover Art: Carrie Hohmann

Author Photo: Talya Chalef

Cover Design: Elizabeth Maines

Printed in the USA on acid-free paper.
Order online: www.finishinglinepress.com
also available on amazon.com

Author inquiries and mail orders:
Finishing Line Press
P. O. Box 1626
Georgetown, Kentucky 40324
U. S. A.

Table of Contents

For Dorothy, the biggest heart I ever loved
& CQ a big heart with legs and shoes

BEFORE MUCH ADO ABOUT NOTHING

When I read a poem
that fucks me up
with its gorgeousness
I don't want to be the poet.
I want to be the poem.
I'm sorry for bumping
into your mom, Kid.
It was summer in NYC.
Little white face, you
craned back your head
to face the accuser.
In the afterlife, I'll be
a poem. Just a plain
sheet of typing paper
bludgeoned with ink.
The one that captures
the tar-green tenderness
in your, eyes, hardened
with daughterly outrage.

60-YEAR SLIDE

I said, 'Sweetheart, the water's already been off.'"
—Nicole Hill

A pipe wrench
tempers serrated teeth
    that bite with
    increasing
    brutality as
    the wrench
    turns

_*_

When she came
to die,
Dorothy did
not bring her
birding books.
As a young
woman, it was
agonizing to
pretend the
doctor's
restriction—
six ounces of
water, per
hour—
was not
torture.

-*-

Tell me the story of Detroit/ The fear mongering debt crisis/
"Grand Bargain" art heist at the DIA/ an INTERACTIVE MAP OF 3,400
HOMES/ SLATED FOR DEMOLITION/
Little Hamtramck house/ where my father was born
clot/ of red blood cells/ now a googlemap of blight/ seat me
in the ghost/ assembly line where/ Richard stood/ a semicentury
cutting steel/ FORD MOTOR COMPANY/ his four boys/ hawked for college

-*-

Race red
steel, 48 in.
reinforced
handle, full
floating
forged hook
jaw. Tail
pierced
with a grommet
for hanging
when not
in use.

-*-

You   watch a woman die,
of thirst,   it changes you.

WHO I LOVE

I am the surgeon
who drugged
and sliced you up.

Inside the hollow
joint, fastened
a porcine whale.

I fell in love
with your
Ulnar Nerve.

Desire, a funny
bone, prattles
over the floor.

INFINITE FISH

Sometimes when my love and I lay senseless
in the woolpack of sleep, I recall the *coma*: nebulous cloud
of ice and dust sublimating around the nucleus of a comet—

and it becomes the fuzz of a workday burned up in commuter traffic
or lost in the Oort Cloud of meetings. When my partner
steps out for work, I get a twinge of losses. Then comes

the plush feeling of domesticity, that infinite fish turning inside me.
On the same night as the Charleston Church Shooting,
I listen to a scientist's recording of a plant dying of thirst.

It sounds like the first drops of rain striking an air conditioner,
then a torrential downpour into nothingness. In America,
it's possible for a white supremacist to sit in a prayer meeting

for an hour before murdering nine black parishioners.
The living ask, *Where do we go to get free? Where do we go to live?*
The human heart weighs as much as a can of Coke.

The line, *Where do we go to get free? Where do we go to live?* is quoted from
"Up Here, From There: In Conversation with Jacob Lawrence" by DéLana R.A.
Dameron and Jessica Lynne in *Arts.Black: A Journal of Art Criticism from Black
Perspectives.*

POEM AFTER MAN:
KITCHEN TABLE

1.
I thought here's a man. Who owns who he is.
Look how natural you move in your animal skin.

2.
Paraffin wax burns at a steady rate of 0.1 g/min, releasing roughly 80 watts.
Low light, we touched each other's faces and shoulders, softened into the quilt.
A dark-furred skyscraper loomed at the window, waiting to be let in to sleep alongside his masters.

4.
My   mother   //laughs// interrupts everything to unbottle hilarity.

You like him as much as a kitchen table?

3.
If we married/ I would decade you/ in the kitchen/ our children's bright specs/ traces of stray crayon/ adorn/ your spalted grooves/ stay while the baby/ sleeps with you cheek/ to cheek/ pendant dreams of the blue-grey seas/ we were born to planet earth/ and to our mothers/ and grew from seed.

10.
"I apologize if you thought this was some kind of trajectory," she said
"Maple," he said.

11.
I took
a record
player
needle
to your
tree
rings

Mozart
based his
master
pieces
on
broken
chords and
arpeggios

I would gladly
surrender
a thousand
years

It played
an
alberti
bass

We
can't be
far off
wanting
a song that
won't
wind
down

Rooted

in place

eyeless

mute

de-eared

waiting

Bright
pluck of
rain
falling
on a
loved one
walking
from
the carport

//oh my love

The
sounds
of our
spring together,
the trees
were listening.

For the beloved.

UNTRACEABLE

The last thing you said to me
was if you do this, I'll never speak
to you again. Until today, I could imagine
your life. Now my thoughts occur in careful,
calculated measure. Late afternoon naps
at my desk chair, head tilted back, it's safe
to conjure your bright smile. As if somehow
by focusing on a tooth, I cannot be torn by it.
I remember your body, politely. Chaste praise
of the curve of your buttock rounding into thigh.
Idiot memory, mine, it's no longer my right to chronicle.
Yet the dark nettles of your frankness have softened
into daydreams of old care packages.
Is this how love ends? A gradual
retirement of the lead hammer
dug into a trench in the seashore.
I say love never leaves us completely.
I say, in gratitude of this life,
I wish a thousand kindnesses on you.
Untraceable, back to me.

BLUE DOG BLUE DOG

Mid-sentence while teaching
a freshman seminar, a stranger

in a blue dog costume enters.
Blue Dog paces in eerily

without saying a word—
mimes his threadbare mitts

for us to carry-on. I search
the shadowbox of mesh

beneath its battered plastic eyes
for any indication of what's next.

Where an ID card should rest,
an empty plastic case swings, freely.

When Blue Dog speaks,
his voice is crushed gravel:

One time I buried a bone.
I buried a bone, then I dug it up.

A part of me leaves my body.
When it's over, he walks out.

Five days later, an Oregon community
college student shoots his English teacher

and nine others. The gunman says,
I've wanted to do this for years.

TANAGER STREET

Home after dark
I listen for the electric
pierce of the television,
for her slipper shuffle.

I wait to hear the tumble
of clothes in the dryer,
the kettle whistle
from the stove.

Not even a vacuum
disturbs the silence.
I am late and want
to be forgiven.

TWIN MOONS

There are no stores
on the moon. Only the dark
centers of the lunar maria.

Missing you isn't so bad.
Thinking about you makes me happy,
the astronaut read from
a crumpled postcard tucked
into his suit.

Early scientists bet their wives
these craters held seas.

An impossible woman
stood on her porch
in Texas.

A dark speck
absorbed the pour
of refrigerator light
from the moon.

Like a fly heavy
with cold, battening
down the latches
on the sheep pens.

THANKSGIVING BREAK 2009

An armed robber holds up the Meijer gas station Saturday,
demands cigarettes and money. Hours later, hits the Rite-Aid
for more cash. By Monday he's unstoppable—
knocking over Huntington Bank in broad daylight,
barefaced and brandishing a grin for security cameras.
Radios belch live coverage of the *Funny Filcher*
robbing a CVS-Pharmacy Tuesday morning, as Barb
waits for my plane to land. One overexcited
resident blurts, *Adrian is the new Manhattan!*
My sister's high school issues a lockdown.
The gunman holds up a clerk at Walmart.
On the move, he revisits the Meijer gas station,
carjacking a pickup truck. Gun leveled
at the woman's face, he hisses, *I'll shoot you
and your baby*. We're all rooting for him.

ROTHKO'S BOY WITH RED BACKPACK

Green yellow black red blue
the boy's socks dug elastic lines
into his shins. "Why's he just standin' there?"

Unmistakably, the voice of grandpa.
The red backpack in the sky leered.
A radio on the counter surged with volume,

prompting a hand to switch it off altogether.
"Nothing wrong with what he's done."
This voice, grandma's.

The red backpack in the sky hung low
with a sharp plumb. "An anvil," the boy
thought and hunched forward under

its weight. Green yellow black red blue
the boy studied his socks. "Oh, he's a good
boy." A voice, maybe an aunt's.

From his vantage point, everyone was a cerise
blur. "Just fell in love, that's all."
The red backpack heaved, as if by habit.

FLEUR D' ORLEANS

Right now
your half smile
pulls me into
a kiss, and I wish
it's winter
so I can steal
out of bed
to clear
the flurries
from your windshield.
While you teach
the sunrise
to praise its silver
lining, I'd coax
our old red car
to blast
the familiar
engine-chant
of heat. Spindrift
already pulling
granules
of my boot
tracks back
into the
snow.

EPIGRAMS FOR DOROTHY

i am the maine coon
you drowned in iron
lake

a fisherman crashed
in after you
but i got held under

-*-

i want you
to be an animal
pancake again

used to be i could detect
the plume of your redbird voice
amidst the figurines' silence

-*-

you haven't phoned
a soul in seven years
i am your ears

it's me, meeko!
the shitzu you put down
i'm waiting on the other side
will you bring gumdrops?

-*-

i am the slum gun vodka
mandatory aneurysm in your brain
get on the floor

if the memories in your cortex
metabolized are they the jules
caterwauling in bloodheat?

_*_

on visits i wriggled
deep into the fresh down
weft of your comforter

a jolly clam
of teeth swam beside
us in a jar

_*_

were you trying to drown yourself
in the lake & needed the cat?
did you see the fisherman?
he never saw the cat

i am the persian cat
you call kitty-doggie
i don't care what you call me
i won't come near you

_*_

i am the letters
your granddaughter wrote.
we lined the pockets
of your winter coat
the bottom of your purse

-*-

i am your neighbor lady
from iron lake. our kids
used to play together
now were roommates
in a nursing home
& we don't know it.

Sarah Sala is a poet and educator with roots in Brooklyn, Michigan. Her poem "Hydrogen" was recently featured in the "Elements" episode of NPR's hit show Radiolab in collaboration with Emotive Fruition. Her awards and honors include: an Academy of American Poets Prize, the Marjorie Rapport Award for Poetry, an Avery Hopwood Award for Nonfiction, and a Roy W. Cowden Memorial Fellowship. She earned her MFA in Poetry from New York University, and is a 2016 Home School Fellow. Her poems appear in *Wreck Park, Atlas Review,* and *The Stockholm Review of Literature.* Visit her at SarahSala.com.